Hello, Beautiful!

Pet Animals

WORLD
BOOK

www.worldbook.com

World Book, Inc.
180 North LaSalle Street, Suite 900
Chicago, Illinois 60601
USA

For information about other World Book
publications, visit our website at
www.worldbook.com or call
1-800-WORLDBK (967-5325).

For information about sales to schools and
libraries, call 1-800-975-3250 (United States),
or 1-800-837-5365 (Canada).

Library of Congress Cataloging-in-Publication
Data for this volume has been applied for.

Hello, Beautiful!
ISBN: 978-0-7166-3567-3 (set, hc.)

Pet Animals
ISBN: 978-0-7166-3574-1 (hc.)

Also available as:
ISBN: 978-0-7166-3584-0 (e-book)

Printed in China by Shenzhen Wing King Tong
Paper Products Co., Ltd., Shenzhen, Guangdong
1st printing July 2018

Staff

Writer: Shawn Brennan

Executive Committee

President
Jim O'Rourke

Vice President and
Editor in Chief
Paul A. Kobasa

Vice President, Finance
Donald D. Keller

Vice President, Marketing
Jean Lin

Vice President,
International Sales
Maksim Rutenberg

Vice President, Technology
Jason Dole

Director, Human Resources
Bev Ecker

Editorial

Director, New Print
Tom Evans

Managing Editor, New Print
Jeff De La Rosa

Senior Editor, New Print
Shawn Brennan

Editor, New Print
Grace Guibert

Librarian
S. Thomas Richardson

Manager, Contracts &
Compliance (Rights &
Permissions)
Loranne K. Shields

Manager, Indexing Services
David Pofelski

Digital

Director, Digital Content
Development
Emily Kline

Director, Digital Product
Development
Erika Meller

Manager, Digital Products
Jonathan Wills

Graphics and Design

Senior Art Director
Tom Evans

Senior Visual
Communications Designer
Melanie Bender

Media Researcher
Media Bledsoe
Rosa

Manufacturing/
Production

Manufacturing Manager
Anne Fritzin

Proofreader
Nathalie Strassheim

Contents

Introduction

Welcome to "Hello, Beautiful!" picture books!

This book is about pet animals. Each book in the "Hello, Beautiful!" series uses large, colorful photographs and a few words to describe our world to children who are not yet reading on their own or are beginning to learn to read. For the benefit of both grown-up and child readers, a picture key is included in the back of the volume to describe each photograph and specific type of animal in more detail.

"Hello, Beautiful!" books can help pre-readers and starting readers get into the habit of having fun with books and learning from them, too. With pre-readers, a grown-up reader (parent, grandparent, librarian, teacher, older brother or sister) can point to the words on each page as he or she speaks them aloud to help the listening child associate the concept of text with the object or idea it describes.

Large, colorful photographs give pre-readers plenty to see while they listen to the reader. If no reader is available, pre-readers can "read" on their own, turning the pages of the book and speaking their own stories about what they see. For new readers, the photographs provide visual hints about the words on the page. Often, these words describe the specific type of animal shown. This animal may not be representative of all species, or types, of that animal.

This book displays some of the wonderful pet animals that are companions to many people. Help inspire love and care for these special and beautiful animals by sharing this "Hello, Beautiful!" book with a child soon.

Canary

Hello, beautiful canary!

You are a cheerful yellow bird.

You love to sing pretty songs—
and we love to hear them!

Cat

Hello, beautiful cat!

You are an American shorthair cat. We love to pet your soft fur.

When you sniff **catnip**, you become very playful!

Dog

Hello, beautiful dog!

You are an Australian terrier.
Some dogs are small like
you. Others are big.

You are a good friend to
people. You wag your tail
when you are happy!

Goldfish

Hello, beautiful goldfish!

You may be red, orange, brown, gray, black, or white. But you all are still called goldfish!

Guinea pig

Hello, beautiful guinea pig!

You are an American guinea pig. You are covered in soft fur. You have a big head, shiny **black** eyes, small ears, and short legs.

You come in many colors. And you are not really a pig!

Hamster

Hello, beautiful hamster!

You are a golden hamster. You are furry. You have a pink nose, bright eyes, and a short tail.

Your cheeks puff out when you fill them up with food!

Hedgehog

Hello, beautiful hedgehog!

You are a four-toed hedgehog. You are covered in pointy prickles!

When you are scared, you roll up into a ball!

Hello, beautiful horse!

You are a Tennessee walking horse. We love to ride you and brush your mane and tail.

Horses have been friends to people for a very long time!

Lizard

Hello, beautiful lizard!

You are a blue-tongued skink.

You have short legs and toes that end in claws.

Your skin is thick, dry, and bumpy. Other animals do not want to eat you!

Rabbit

Hello, beautiful rabbit!

You are a Standard Rex rabbit. You have long ears and a short, fluffy tail.

It is fun to watch you hop about. We like to feed you carrots as a special treat!

Snake

Hello, beautiful ssssssssnake!

You are a corn snake.
You wriggle your long body
to move over the ground.

You stick your tongue
out and pull it back in.
This is how you smell!

Tarantula

Hello, beautiful tarantula!

You are a Mexican redknee tarantula. You are a giant spider. You have a furry body and furry legs.

You tickle us as you crawl up an arm!

Picture Key

Learn more about these animal pets! Use the picture keys below to learn where each pet came from, how big it grows, and what kinds of foods are best to feed it!

Pages 6-7 Canary

This is a domestic canary (*kuh NAIR ee*). This bird was brought to Europe from the Canary Islands, where it still lives in the wild. Canaries grow up to about 8 inches (20 centimeters) long. Pet canaries should be fed seeds, fruits, and vegetables. The bird should always have fresh water available for drinking and bathing.

Pages 8-9 Cat

The American shorthair probably developed from cats originally brought to the American Colonies by Europeans. The breed weighs about 6 to 15 pounds (3 to 7 kilograms). All cats need a balanced diet. Your cat should be fed high-quality commercial cat food. Fresh drinking water should always be available.

Pages 10-11 Dog

The Australian terrier originated in Australia about 1885. The breed weighs about 12 to 14 pounds (5.4 to 6.4 kilograms). Dogs require different kinds of foods during the various stages of their lives. Your dog should be fed high-quality commercial dog food. Fresh drinking water should always be available.

Pages 12-13 Goldfish

This is a domestic goldfish. Domestic goldfish developed from the wild crucian carp, which is native to China and other parts of Asia. Domestic goldfish measure in length from 2 or 3 inches (5 or 8 centimeters) to almost 2 feet (60 centimeters). The largest varieties can weigh 6 ½ pounds (3 kilograms) or more. Young, active goldfish should be fed twice a day. Older goldfish should be fed only once a day. Give only as much food as the fish can eat in a few minutes. Owners should use commercially prepared fish food, occasionally supplementing that food with plant material.

Pages 14-15 Guinea pig

Guinea (*GIHN ee*) pigs are from South America. They measure from 10 to 14 inches (25 to 36 centimeters) long and weigh from 2 to 3 pounds (0.9 to 1.4 kilograms). Their diet should contain commercial food pellets and hay, supplemented with fruits and vegetables. Food and clean water should be available at all times.

Pages 16-17 Hamster

Hamsters are native to Asia and Europe. Golden hamsters measure about 7 inches (18 centimeters) long and have a tail ½ inch (13 millimeters) long. The animals weigh about 4 ounces (112 grams). Hamsters may be given many kinds of food, including fruits, greens, raw vegetables, small grains, and some meat. Fresh water should be available at all times.

Hedgehog

Hello, beautiful hedgehog!

You are a four-toed hedgehog. You are covered in pointy prickles!

When you are scared, you roll up into a ball!

Horse

Hello, beautiful horse!

You are a Tennessee walking horse. We love to ride you and brush your mane and tail.

Horses have been friends to people for a very long time!

Lizard

Hello, beautiful lizard!

You are a blue-tongued skink.

You have short legs and toes that end in claws.

Your skin is thick, dry, and bumpy. Other animals do not want to eat you!

Pages 18-19 Hedgehog

The four-toed hedgehog lives across Central Africa. It grows to about 6 to 10 inches (15 to 25 centimeters) in length. Hedgehogs in the wild eat insects, snakes, small mammals, birds, and birds' eggs. Commercial hedgehog food may also be fed to pet hedgehogs. Fresh water should be available at all times.

Pages 20-21 Horse

The Tennessee walking horse developed in Middle Tennessee, in the United States, in the late 1700's. The breed measures 15 to 16 hands (60 to 64 inches, 150 to 163 centimeters) from the ground to the highest point of the *withers* (ridge between the shoulder bones). It weighs 900 to 1,200 pounds (410 to 540 kilograms). Horses eat grass, grain, and hay. A horse needs food at least three times a day. Most horses require from 10 to 12 gallons (38 to 45 liters) of fresh, clean water daily.

Pages 22-23 Lizard

Most species of blue-tongued skinks *(skihngks)* are found in Australia. One species is found in New Guinea and on some islands of Indonesia. Most species of blue-tongued skinks grow from 12 to 24 inches (30 to 61 centimeters) in length. They generally eat small insects, snails, slugs, flowers, fruit, and berries. Skinks may also be fed canned and dry dog food.

Rabbit

Hello, beautiful rabbit!

You are a Standard Rex rabbit. You have long ears and a short, fluffy tail.

It is fun to watch you hop about. We like to feed you carrots as a special treat!

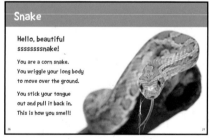

Snake

Hello, beautiful sssssssnake!

You are a corn snake. You wriggle your long body to move over the ground.

You stick your tongue out and pull it back in. This is how you smell!

Tarantula

Hello, beautiful tarantula!

You are a Mexican redknee tarantula. You are a giant spider. You have a furry body and furry legs.

You tickle us as you crawl up an arm!

Pages 24-25 Rabbit

The Standard Rex rabbit was first bred in France. It weighs about 7 ½ to 10 ½ pounds (3.5 to 5 kilograms). Pet rabbits should be fed high-quality commercial rabbit pellets. They may also be fed small amounts of bread, tender twigs and sprouts, and such fruits and vegetables as apples, cabbage, cauliflower, leaf lettuce, spinach, and turnips. Carrots should only be given sparingly. Fresh water should be available at all times.

Pages 26-27 Snake

The corn snake is a common, nonpoisonous snake of eastern North America. Adult corn snakes can reach up to 72 inches (180 centimeters) long. However, most measure about 24 to 48 inches (60 to 120 centimeters) long. It feeds mainly on birds, eggs, frogs, lizards, and rodents.

Pages 28-29 Tarantula

The Mexican redknee tarantula *(tuh RAN chuh luh)* is a nonpoisonous tarantula. It is native to the Pacific Coast of Mexico, but can now also be found in Costa Rica and the southwestern United States. An adult reaches up to 5 ½ inches (14 centimeters) with its legs extended. It mainly eats insects. But it will also eat frogs, mice, and other small animals.

Index